D1207350

FIGHTING FORCES IN THE AIR

SUPER HORNET F/A-18E/F

LYNN STONE

www.rourkepublishing.com

PHOTO CREDITS: All photos courtesy of the U.S. Navy

Title page: *A Super Hornet is directed on a catapult aboard the* U.S.S. John C. Stennis.

Editor: Frank Sloan

Library of Congress Cataloging-in-Publication Data

Stone, Lynn M.
  Super Hornet F/A-18E/F / Lynn M. Stone.
      p. cm. -- (Fighting forces in the air)
  Includes bibliographical references and index.
  ISBN 1-59515-179-6 (hardcover)
  1. Hornet (Jet fighter plane) I. Title. II. Series: Stone, Lynn M. Fighting forces in the air.
  UG1242.F5S793 2004
  623.74'64--dc22
                                          2004011742

Printed in the USA

CG/CG

TABLE OF CONTENTS

THE F/A-18E/F SUPER HORNET

The F/A-18E/F Super Hornet is the U.S. Navy's newest and best **multi-role** fighter aircraft. Super Hornets fly from the deck of Navy aircraft carriers. They are fast, highly **maneuverable**, and they are loaded with flying features for top performance and pilot control.

The Super Hornet performs several missions for the Navy. Its designation as an F/A aircraft refers to its role as both fighter (F) and attack (A) aircraft. The Super Hornet can be equipped quickly to be an air-to-air combat fighter, air-to-surface attack jet, or both.

A Super Hornet launches from one of four steam-powered catapults aboard the U.S.S. Kitty Hawk.

▲

In tight formation, Super Hornets roar over the western Pacific Ocean after launch from the Nimitz Carrier Strike Group.

As a true fighter plane, the Super Hornet can engage and destroy enemy aircraft in the air. As attack aircraft, Super Hornets can attack targets on land or sea, day or night. For night missions, F/A-18E/F pilots wear night goggles. Night goggle systems use **infrared** technology so that pilots can see images in darkness.

In addition, the Super Hornet can provide close-in weapons support for friendly ground and sea forces. It can also be used as a high-flying **reconnaissance** aircraft to spy on enemy positions.

F/A-18E/F Characteristics

Function: Multi-role fighter and attack aircraft

Primary Contractors: Boeing (McDonnell Douglas Aerospace) and Northrop Grumman

Power Source: Two F414-GE-400 turbofan engines

Thrust: 22,000 pounds (9,977 kilograms) per engine

Length: 60.3 feet (18.5 meters)

Height: 16 feet (4.87 meters)

Wingspan: 44.9 feet (13.68 meters)

Speed: More than 1,350 miles per hour (2,160 kilometers per hour)

Ceiling: Above 50,000 feet (15,240 meters)

Maximum Takeoff Weight: 66,000 pounds (29,932 kilograms)

Range: More than 1,840 miles (2,944 kilometers)

Combat Range: approximately 1,450 miles (2,348 kilometers)

Crew: One (F/A-18E) or two (F/A-18F)

Date Deployed: 2001

The F/A-18E Super Hornet is a single seat airplane. The F/A-18F is a two-seater. They are the latest versions of the F-18 series that began with the model A and B Hornets. The F-18A/B versions, and more recently the F-18C/D versions, were simply known as Hornets, not *Super* Hornets. The original Hornets began regular military service in the early 1980s.

The two-seat Super Hornet is primarily used for attack, air control missions, and reconnaissance work. It can also be used for training flights.

An F/A-18C Hornet makes a final approach to its landing aboard the U.S.S. Harry Truman.

The Super Hornet has several advantages over earlier F-18s. The Super Hornet is about 25 percent larger, but contains fewer structural parts. That makes it easier to maintain and repair. The Super Hornet has greater fuel capacity—a third more in its internal tanks—for a longer flying range. With greater size and strength, the Super Hornet carries heavier payloads—up to 9,000 pounds (4,054 kg) of fuel, weapons, and equipment. The Super Hornet is slightly faster than older F-18s and accelerates more quickly. The Super Hornet also has more firepower than previous Hornets.

Internally the Super Hornet is a much-improved aircraft, too. It is loaded with state-of-the-art electronic systems. And as flight and weapons systems improve, they can be installed on the Super Hornets. The airplane was designed with room for growth in its **avionics** and weapons systems.

Sailors push an F/A-18E Super Hornet on the U.S.S. Abraham Lincoln's *flight deck.* ▶

An aviation electronics specialist checks avionics in a Hornet cockpit aboard the U.S.S. George Washington. ▶

▲

An F/A-18F Super Hornet lands on the deck of the
U.S.S. Kitty Hawk.

FLYING THE SUPER HORNET

CHAPTER TWO

Unlike land-based aircraft, the Super Hornet flies from the deck of an aircraft carrier. After a mission, the F-18E/F returns to the ship.

An aircraft carrier is not long enough for an airplane to make its usual takeoff from a standing start. The Super Hornet and other carrier-based fighters are launched into the air by a **catapult.**

A Super Hornet begins its takeoff in catapult position on the carrier flight deck. The pilot revs the engines to full throttle while a device holds the Super Hornet's nose gear, preventing it from moving forward. When the pilot is ready for launch, the catapult is fired. The nose gear is released and the airplane rockets the length of the deck and into the air.

FACT FILE ★

WITH THE CATAPULT BOOST, THE PLANE GOES FROM ZERO TO ABOUT 170 MILES PER HOUR (272 KM/H) INTO THE AIR IN TWO SECONDS!

▲
A Super Hornet launches past the flight deck officer.

The Super Hornet's twin turbofan engines produce 35 percent more **thrust** than the Hornet's engines. Once airborne, a Super Hornet can fly at speeds beyond 1,350 miles per hour (2,160 km/h), or **Mach** 1.8. (Mach 1 represents the speed of sound.) At an altitude of approximately 40,000 feet (12,192 m) the speed of sound is about 750 miles per hour (1,200 km/h). The speed of sound is slower at lower altitudes where the air is denser, thus slowing the speed that sound—or an airplane— can travel.

FACT FILE ★

SUPER HORNETS AND OTHER SUPERSONIC MILITARY AIRCRAFT USUALLY FLY AT SPEEDS LESS THAN THE SPEED OF SOUND.

▲ *One of the "Black Aces" of Strike Fighter Squadron 41, a Super Hornet streaks over the Pacific Ocean.*

Landing a Super Hornet on the deck of an aircraft carrier requires great skill and communication with the flight deck. A Super Hornet approaches the carrier deck at the slowest possible speed, about 130 miles per hour (208 km/h). The approaching plane drops a steel hook from its tail end. As the plane touches down on the carrier, that **tailhook** catches one of four steel cables—called arresting wires—stretched across the deck. The cable that catches the tailhook stretches a short distance with the plane's forward speed and stops the aircraft.

A Super Hornet pilot has at his or her fingertips a wide range of flight systems. They are designed to help a pilot fly, attack, and avoid being attacked. The Super Hornet cockpit has a touch-sensitive control display. It has a larger, multi-purpose color display that shows additional data and three other display screens. The cockpit also has a digital color map.

▲ *The tailhook of a Super Hornet catches an arresting wire aboard the* U.S.S. John C. Stennis.

◀

Technicians check Global Positioning Systems (GPS) in a Super Hornet on the deck of the U.S.S. Kitty Hawk.

▼ *The cockpit of a Super Hornet brims with high-tech electronics.*

For information about the world beyond their cockpits, Super Hornet pilots have APG-73 radar systems. The system has several modes. One or another gives a pilot information about objects in the air and objects on the ground. The Information and Electronic Warfare System provides more information and manages a series of defensive devices. The ALE-47 **countermeasures** system can dispense **chaff**, flares, or decoys into the air. These measures can confuse enemy missiles and radar systems.

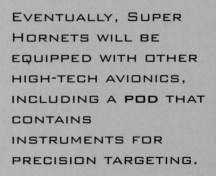

FACT FILE ★

EVENTUALLY, SUPER HORNETS WILL BE EQUIPPED WITH OTHER HIGH-TECH AVIONICS, INCLUDING A **POD** THAT CONTAINS INSTRUMENTS FOR PRECISION TARGETING.

▲
Navy weapons handlers carry an advanced medium-range, air-to-air missile to a Super Hornet.

FIREPOWER

The Super Hornet has 11 weapons stations. The plane can carry a variety of missiles and bombs. As a fighter aircraft, the Super Hornet can unleash such air-to-air weapons as the AIM-9 Sidewinder, AIM-7 Sparrow, and AIM-120 AMRAAM missiles. For surface attack the Super Hornet can launch the GPS- and computer-guided JDAM (Joint Direct Attack Munition), the precision-guided JSOW (Joint Standoff Weapon), and the JASSM (Joint Air-to-Surface Standoff Missile).

Weapons in the standoff group can be used to attack a target from a greater distance than ever before, which is why they're called "standoff." The JSOW, for example, can be dropped from a distance of 18 to 70 miles (29 to 112 km) away from the target, depending on the Super Hornet's altitude. High altitude permits a greater weapon-release range.

▲ *Weapons handlers aboard the* U.S.S. Nimitz *lift an AIM-120 air-to-air missile from a weapons skid. The AIM-120 is a new generation all-weather weapon.*

The F/A-18E/F has a new, lightweight Gatling gun, the General Dynamics M61A2. Built into the Super Hornet nose, its rotating barrels can fire up to 6,000 bullets per minute.

The Navy will soon equip its Super Hornets with the HOBS (High Off-Boresight Seeker) weapons system. For the pilot, it's like having a TV screen built into the helmet visor.

▶

A sailor attaches a fin to a 500-pound (227-kg) GBU-12 laser-guided bomb before attaching it to a Super Hornet.

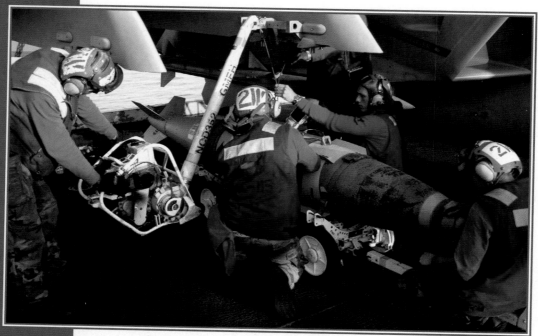

▲ *Aviation weapons men attach a 2,000-pound (907-kg) Joint Direct Attack Munition (JDAM) to the wing of a Super Hornet during Operation Iraqi Freedom.*

The visor display gives the pilot a targeting device that can be used to aim sensors and weapons wherever the pilot is looking. With this system, the pilot can aim radar, air-to-air missiles, infrared sensors, and air-to-surface weapons by simply pointing his or her head at the target and pressing a switch!

The pilot will also be able to view other data, such as air speed and altitude, while keeping "heads up" during air combat. The system includes the AIM-9X missile, a weapon that can destroy any airborne enemy the pilot can see. The pilot will not even have to maneuver the aircraft to fire the AIM-9X.

▲
An F-18A Hornet with the Nimitz Carrier Strike Group flies over the western Pacific.

The Super Hornet (foreground) is gradually replacing the F-14 Tomcat (left) on American aircraft carriers.

CHAPTER FOUR

The original F-18A/Bs were built to replace aging and **obsolete** F-4 Phantom IIs and A-7s. The first F-18As became combat-ready in 1983. After more than 400 F-18A/Bs were built, the advanced F-18C/Ds arrived in 1987.

The first use of a Hornet in combat was against Libyan radar and missile sites in 1986. During Operation Desert Storm in 1991, American and Canadian F-18s attacked targets in and near Iraq around the clock. On the first day of the war, two F18-As shot down a pair of Iraqi MiG fighters.

The Super Hornet, successor to earlier Hornet models and the F-14 Tomcat, began sea trials in January, 1997. The first combat-ready Super Hornets were deployed in July, 2002, aboard the aircraft carrier *U.S.S. Abraham Lincoln*. In November, 2002, Super Hornets flew an attack mission against Iraqi targets during Operation Southern Watch. They flew combat missions again in the spring of 2003 during Operation Iraqi Freedom.

▲
A Super Hornet is directed to one of a carrier's catapults prior to launch.

FLYING INTO THE FUTURE

The U.S. Navy will purchase a minimum of 460 Super Hornets. The airplanes will be built at least into 2009. The exact number of Super Hornets ordered will depend somewhat on the progress of another fighter aircraft, the F-35 Joint Strike Fighter. The JSF is being developed by the Air Force and Navy together.

Meanwhile, as new **squadrons** of Super Hornets become available, they are being assigned to Navy aircraft carriers. Eventually, 20 squadrons will be ready for combat. Each aircraft carrier at sea during any given time will have two squadrons of Super Hornets—a squadron each of F/A-18Es and F/A-18Fs.

The Super Hornet's great capacity for new hardware and software systems will keep it flying well into the future beyond 2009.

Glossary

avionics (AY vee ON iks) — the electronic systems and devices used in aviation

catapult (KAT uh PULLT) — a device that rockets an airplane from an aircraft carrier deck into the air

chaff (CHAFF) — small metal strips released into the air to confuse radar systems

countermeasures (KAUNT ur MEZH urz) — any number of strategies and systems used to avoid being struck by enemy fire

infrared (IN fruh RED) — (also known as *thermal radiation* or *infrared rays*) the invisible-to-the-naked-eye energy rays given off by any warm object, such as a human being, battle tank, or airplane; invisible heat rays that can be detected by special instruments

Mach (MAWK) — a high speed expressed by a Mach number; Mach 1 is the speed of sound

maneuverable (muh NYUV uh ra bul) — able to make changes in direction and position for a specific purpose

multi-role (MUL tee ROLL) — capable of being used in more than one way

obsolete (OB suh leet) — no longer current; out-of-date

pod (PAWD) — a rounded compartment in which various electronic or other devices may be kept on an aircraft body

reconnaissance (ruh KON uh zawns) — the gathering of information about a foe; the information gathered

squadrons (SKWAD runz) — working units of 12 military airplanes

supersonic (SU per SON ik) — any speed above the speed of sound

tailhook (TALE HOOK) — the steel hook used by a carrier-based airplane to grasp an arresting wire when the plane lands on the carrier deck

thrust (THRUST) — the forward force of an object; the force produced by an aircraft engine

INDEX

FURTHER READING

Graham, Ian. *Attack Fighters*. Heinemann, 2003

Holden, Henry M. *Navy Combat Aircraft and Pilots*. Enslow, 2002

Sweetman, Bill. *Strike Fighters: The F/A-18E/F Super Hornets*. Capstone, 2001

WEBSITES TO VISIT

http://www.chinfo.navy.mil/navpalib/factfile/aircraft/air-fa18.html

http://www.boeing.com/defense-space/military/fa18/fa18.htm

ABOUT THE AUTHOR

Lynn M. Stone is the author of more than 400 children's books. He is a talented natural history photographer as well. Lynn, a former teacher, travels worldwide to photograph wildlife in its natural habitat.